SAINTS IN S
CHURC

John Salmon

SUFFOLK HISTORIC CHURCHES TRUST
1981

THE SUFFOLK HISTORIC CHURCHES TRUST

This booklet is published and sold to assist the work of the **Suffolk Historic Churches Trust** whose publications include *Suffolk Churches — A Pocket Guide* and a series of booklets edited by John Blatchly on special topics, which include:

1. *Medieval Tiles in Suffolk Churches* David Sherlock
2. *Bells and Bellringing in Suffolk* Ranald Clouston and George Pipe
3. *Saints in Suffolk Churches* John Salmon
4. *Benches and Stalls in Suffolk Churches* John Agate

A further booklet on Victorian Stained Glass is in preparation.

The Trust's overriding aim is the preservation, for the purposes for which they were built, of Suffolk's renowned heritage of historic churches and chapels. Since its formation in December, 1973, building costs have soared with inflation. In many cases, State Aid has come to the rescue, indeed Suffolk's churches already have been promised nearly £1,250,000 by the Department of the Environment. Usually, these grants are to cover half the total cost leaving the parishes themselves to find the other half by charitable gifts of one sort or another. Therefore it is more important than ever that we should help parishes to raise their share; they cannot manage this alone.

So far, we have promised £112,000 to 208 churches in grants varying from £50 to £1,500, but there are 500 churches and chapels in Suffolk nearly all in need of extensive repair.

We need your help through gifts or subscriptions to the Trust, better still a covenanted gift as we then can reclaim the Income Tax. For further information or a membership form please apply to the **Hon. Secretary, Mrs. J. N. Agate, The Old Rectory, Chattisham, Ipswich IP8 3PY (Tel: Hintlesham 306).**

ISBN 0 9505385 3 1

Photoset in Great Britain by
Rowland Phototypesetting Ltd, Bury St. Edmunds, Suffolk
and printed by Frieson Printing Services, Brentford, Middlesex

CONTENTS

The cover shows the painted panels of the screen at Eye. From the left the saints are Helen, Edmund, Ursula, Henry VI, Dorothy, Barbara, Agnes, Edward the Confessor, John the Evangelist, Catherine, William of Norwich, Lucy, Blaise (?), Cecilia. The last, now effaced, was probably Peter.

Photographs of Eye screen by courtesy of International Computers Limited.

BIBLIOGRAPHY

M. D. Anderson, *A Saint at Stake* (1964): deals with St. William of Norwich.

Francis Bond, *Dedications of English Churches – Ecclesiastical symbolism: Saints and Emblems* (1914).

Tancred Borenius, *St. Thomas Becket in Art* (1932).

H. Munro Cautley, *Suffolk Churches* (1937).

Rev. J. W. Draper, 'Hoxne and St. Edmund' in *Diss Antiquarian Society News Letter*, No. 15 (Spring, 1979).

M. Carey Evans, *The Legend of St. William Boy-Martyr of Norwich* (n.d.) (pamphlet).

D. H. Farmer, *The Oxford Dictionary of Saints* (1978).

V. and H. Hell, *The Great Pilgrimage of the Middle Ages* (*the Road to St. James of Compostela*) (1964).

B. Houghton, *St. Edmund – King and Martyr* (1970).

M. R. James, *Suffolk and Norfolk* (1930) – valuable for its detailed iconographical index.

J. Salmon, 'St. Christopher in Medieval Art and Life' (*Journal of the British Archaeological Association*, vol. for 1936).

N. Scarfe, 'The Body of St. Edmund' (*Proceedings of the Suffolk Institute of Archaeology*, vol. XXXI, 1970).

Suffolk Historic Churches Trust (various authors) *Suffolk Churches* (1977).

L. E. Tanner, Some Representations of St. Edward the Confessor in Westminster Abbey and Elsewhere (*Journal of the British Archaeological Association*, vol. XV, 1952).

E. W. Tristram, *English Wallpainting of the Fourteenth Century* (1954), mainly for the Thornham Parva retable.

J. C. Wall, *Medieval Wallpaintings* (n.d.).

D. Whitelock, 'Fact and Fiction in the Legend of St. Edmund' (*Proceedings of the Suffolk Institute of Archaeology*, vol. XXXI (1970).)

E. Carlton Williams, 'Mural Paintings of St. Catherine in England' (*Journal of the British Archaeological Association*, vol. XIX (1956), 'Mural Paintings of St. George in England', *op. cit.* vol. XII, (1949).).

INTRODUCTION

If you could take H. G. Wells' Time Machine and pedal yourself back some five hundred years to a day in 1480, and you then dismounted and went into the nearest village church, the first thing that would strike you would be the richness of colour in glass and wallpaintings, on screens and in roofs. If in this particular church there were a good deal of wallspace it would be covered with wallpaintings; probably opposite the main door a giant St. Christopher, patron saint of travellers, often quite close to him, as at Bradfield Combust and Troston, St. George, patron saint of England, above the chancel arch a Doom and elsewhere (as formerly at Bardwell, Belton and Kentford) the morality of the Three Living and the Three Dead Kings, a subject which seems to have been popular in East Anglia. Three pleasure loving young kings are out hunting and they meet three skeletons. The kings cry out, "I am afeared, lo! what I see, me thinketh it be devils three", to which the skeletons reply, "I was well fair, such shalt thou be, for God's love be warned by me".

Notice I use the term wallpainting for, after a few experiments of its use in the 12th century, for example at Clayton in Sussex and Kempley in Gloucestershire, the fresco treatment was apparently found unsuitable in our damp climate and the wallpainting technique was universally employed. In simple terms the difference is that in a fresco the paint is applied while the plaster on the wall is still damp so that the two are integrated, while in tempera wallpainting the plaster is allowed to dry before the painting is made. These paintings were blotted out or otherwise destroyed at the Reformation or in Puritan times and were often replaced by paintings of black-letter texts or the Commandments or the Creed, generally set in a painted frame. These in their turn have almost entirely disappeared, those at Great Cornard in the present century, though a few remain as at Weston. However, particularly since Professor E. W. Tristram in the 1920s and 1930s roused interest in our medieval wall paintings, more and more are being uncovered and skilfully treated for preservation. Thus the removal of the decayed woodwork at the east end of Brent Eleigh Church in 1960 revealed an almost perfect Crucifixion with the attendant figures of the Virgin Mary and St. John, with the graceful sway found in figures of *c.* 1300, while a splendid St. Christopher and traces of other paintings came to light at Grundisburgh in 1956. There are more surviving wall paintings in Suffolk (together with Norfolk and Essex) than elsewhere in England for a very simple reason. One of the iniquitous habits of Victorian restorers was to strip the inside surface of the walls of an old church of their plaster covering, thus revealing the fussy surface of the stonework which was never meant to be seen, and destroying all traces of wall paintings which might survive under later layers of plaster. In Suffolk the walls of almost all our pre-Reformation churches are built of flint and not even the worst of the Victorian restorers went to the length of exposing flintwork on the inside, so in most of our Suffolk churches many layers of plaster still remain on the walls, offering the possibility of new discoveries of paintings in the future.

Many of our Suffolk churches were entirely or largely rebuilt sometime in the two hundred years immediately before the Reformation, between 1340 and 1540, through the wealth coming from trade and commerce, particularly in woollen cloth which at that time made East Anglia one of the most prosperous parts of England. Thus a church like Long Melford or, on a much more modest scale, Gipping, when seen from the south, shows a succession of great Perpendicular windows with little wall space between and the saints (and much else) formerly depicted in wallpaintings were now shown in stained glass. But glass was easily destroyed by such Puritan fanatics as William Dowsing, Parliamentary visitor for Suffolk in the Commonwealth, and much disappeared too by sheer neglect in the 18th and early 19th centuries. Denston now has one window of old glass and David Elisha Davy, visiting the church in 1814, recorded several more windows which have since disappeared. But some remain, all fragmentary. Thus at Combs there are some scenes from the life of St. Margaret, while at Long Melford among several secular panels of kneeling donors are figures of St. Edmund and other saints.

Rood screens are a more fruitful source for the searcher after pictures of medieval saints. The upright panels at the base of a screen were ideal settings for figures of saints, one to each panel. A remarkably well preserved set survives at Eye, though the draughtsmanship is not of such a high standard as for example on the screen at Southwold. The Eye painter was not good at faces. Bench ends more often depicted animals or the Seven Deadly Sins as at Blythburgh, or everyday country scenes like the thatcher and haymaker at Ixworth Thorpe, but occasionally saints are found as at Athelington: St. Margaret, St. Jude, St. John, St. James the Great and so on, though here, as at Wilby and Woolpit, some are very good 19th century reproductions.

Rarely were the names of saints inscribed owing to the low level of literacy, but everyone could recognise St. Peter because he was always shown holding the Keys of Heaven, while St. Christopher always carried the Christ Child and St. Catherine held the wheel she was tortured on.

Many saints are also to be found in 19th and 20th century glass, which is of very varying merit, and these I have almost entirely omitted. Thus all the examples of saints I give are pre-Reformation unless it is definitely stated to the contrary. Only one church shows extensive 20th century wall painting, that of St. Christopher accompanied by aeroplane and motor car, at Lound, the work of the late Sir Ninian Comper.

My main problem has been which saints to include. Here are some reasons for my choice. I have included saints with local connections such as St. Edmund, St. Ethelbert, St. Felix, and St. William of Norwich. St. Petronilla is included because in Suffolk she had something of a local cult. St. Christopher and St. George, and to a lesser extent some other saints, must be included for their very great popularity. To have included all the twelve apostles would have necessitated excluding too many other saints, so I have contented myself with St. Peter and St. James the Great, the latter partly because he is the patron saint of our Cathedral at Bury St. Edmunds. St. Blaise figures because he was the patron saint of wool-combers and so connected with the former very profitable Suffolk woollen cloth trade. Others are included because they are fairly often met with in Suffolk churches or in a few cases purely for reasons of personal interest. One of my favourites, Sir John Schorne, was not even officially canonised. With equal justification another author would in all probability have made quite a different selection.

It may be that I have missed some pre-Reformation representations in Suffolk churches of the saints I have dealt with. I should be very pleased to hear of any additions.

Naturally over the years, in the days before printing, the legends of the saints were embellished and embroidered. It may be said, however, that they were crystallised in *The Golden Legend*, compiled by James of Voragine who was Bishop of Genoa and died in 1298. This work became very popular. It was translated from Latin into French in the 14th century and in 1483 Caxton translated and printed *The Golden Legend* in English. In most instances I have used this version of the story of individual saints. The popularity of saints in pre-Reformation days was, of course, primarily due to the belief in their power to intercede with the Almighty on behalf of individuals, thus whether in painting or glass, stonecarving or wood-carving, they dominated a medieval church.

Except in a few obvious cases all places mentioned in the text are in Suffolk unless otherwise stated. I should like to thank Mr G. F. Cordy of Felixstowe for taking the excellent black and white photographs especially for this book, and Mr Norman Scarfe and Mr Peter Northeast for his helpful comments and suggestions on the draft.

St. Blaise. Spring parclose screen at Lavenham.

ST. BARBARA

St. Barbara is said to have been martyred about the year 303 in the persecution under Maximian. Legend has it that she was shut up in a tower by her father so as to avoid the attentions of admiring suitors. By some means she became a Christian and persuaded some workmen to add a third window in honour of the Trinity to a cistern or bathhouse her father was building. Her father was furious and handed her over to a judge who, after Barbara had been tortured, condemned her to death. Her father slew her himself whereupon he was struck by lightning and died. Thus Barbara became the patron saint of those in danger of sudden death, such as miners and gunners. She is depicted holding a tower (her usual attribute) on the panel paintings of the screens in the neighbouring churches of Eye and Yaxley, and in a wall painting at Hessett. No medieval church in Suffolk is dedicated to her.

ST. BLAISE

In his will dated 1523 Thomas Spring III directed his 'body to be buried in the Church of Lavenh'm before the awter of Saint Kateryn where I will be made a tombe with a parclose thereabout at the discretion of myn executors'. A parclose screen divides a chapel from nave and aisle. Thomas Spring, whose father and grandfather bore the same christian name, was an extremely wealthy cloth merchant; in fact he was called 'The Rich Clothier'. The parclose screen at Lavenham survives at the east end of the north aisle of the nave and in view of Thomas Spring's trade it is very appropriate that on its south-east corner post there is a small standing figure of St. Blaise recognisable by the wool comb he is holding. St. Blaise is supposed to have been bishop of Sebaste in Armenia in the early 4th century and to have been martyred by being torn by woolcombs and then beheaded. Thus he became the patron saint of woolcombers. Considering the importance of the wool and cloth trade in Suffolk it is surprising he is not found more often. A figure on the screen at Eye is generally accepted as St. Blaise, but he holds no woolcomb, so the identification must be open to doubt. St. Blaise is also sometimes shown holding a taper as well as a wool comb, presumably because when he was in prison a woman whose son he had healed by removing a fishbone from his throat brought him food and candles. For this reason, on St. Blaise's day (February 3) people suffering from throat diseases sought alleviation by having two candles placed close to their throat.

St. Catherine. Spring parclose screen at Lavenham.

ST. CATHERINE

According to legend Catherine was a well educated girl of noble birth. When she was eighteen a decree was issued by the Emperor Maximinus (or Maxentius in the *Golden Legend* and later versions) that all his subjects should sacrifice to pagan gods. Catherine refused and refuted the emperor's arguments and those of learned philosophers whom she converted to Christianity. St. Catherine was scourged and imprisoned but to no effect. The Emperor then offered her marriage but she replied, 'Christ also offered himself to me. He in sooth is my only spouse', a scene often found in Flemish pictures but not in English medieval art. So the Emperor ordered that she should be tortured on wheels which were miraculously broken and she was finally taken outside the walls of Alexandria and executed. Angels then took her body to Mount Sinai for burial. This was said to have taken place in 307. Her cult began in the 9th century with the discovery of her body and its reburial in the monastic church on Mount Sinai. The cult spread rapidly throughout Europe, doubtless latterly helped by the crusaders, and she became as popular in England as elsewhere. She became the patron saint of workers who used wheels such as wheelwrights, millers and spinners, also of girls because of her mystic marriage to Christ and of philosophers and apologists because of her success in dispute with the Emperor and subsequently with the fifty philosophers whom she converted.

At Sporle in Norfolk no fewer than twenty-seven scenes in the Passion of St. Catherine are depicted in late 14th century wallpainting, now rather faint. A shorter series showing only four scenes was uncovered in 1853 at Bardwell Church and promptly covered up again, but fortunately not before copies had been made by Hamlet Watling whose drawings are now in Christchurch Museum, Ipswich. More often she occurs as a single figure recognised by the wheel (often shown as broken) and sometimes a sword (signifying her martyrdom) that she is holding. St. Catherine with her wheel together with St. Blaise are carved on the Spring parclose screen in the north aisle of Lavenham Church, both appropriate as the Springs were wealthy clothiers. There is an early wallpainting (about 1300) of St. Catherine at Little Wenham Church and another at Thornham Parva. St. Catherine and her wheel are also found carved on fonts at Stowlangtoft (early 14th century) and Nettlestead (early 15th century) and on a bench end at Ufford. There are also figures of the saint in late medieval glass (often in tracery lights) at Blythburgh, Herringfleet, Hawstead (an attractive rayed roundel of yellow stained glass), Long Melford (here she has both the broken wheel and sword and is depicted crowned, dressed in white and seated), Risby and Yaxley. She is also painted on the screens at Eye, Westhall (again with both wheel and sword) and Yaxley, but surely the most attractive St. Catherine in Suffolk is on the painted retable of about 1300 in Thornham Parva Church. A major work of art, its origins

St. Catherine with her wheel from the Thornham Parva retable.

are unknown, but before 1778 it was at Rookery Farm, Stradbroke where the Roman Catholic family of Fox used it in an attic chapel. Thereafter it was preserved at Thornham Hall till in 1927 Lord Henniker presented it to Thornham Parva Church. St. Catherine is shown crowned with her brown hair beneath a transparent veil. She holds an unbroken wheel in her right hand. Notice the long delicate fingers of her disengaged left hand. She wears a close-fitting dark green garment and over it, and, casually worn, a red cloak with white lining. The background consists of green squares each with a golden fleur-de-lis in relief arranged in chequer pattern with golden gesso-covered squares.

15th century bells in the churches of Bildeston (the tower of which suddenly collapsed in 1975) and Stowlangtoft have identical inscriptions, 'Subveniat digna donantibus hanc Katerina' (May noble Catherine help the givers of this bell). A bell at Groton is inscribed 'Wm Chamberlain 1426 Sancta Katerina Deo Pro Nobis'. Only two medieval Suffolk churches, out of a total of sixty-two in the whole country, are dedicated to St. Catherine: Flempton and Ringshall.

ST. CHRISTOPHER

As early as 452 a church in Bythinia was dedicated to St. Christopher, but at that time the story of the saint was a simple one. It was not until the 12th century that a German poet gave it the romantic form familiar to us, and in this form James of Voragine, Bishop of Genoa, incorporated it in his *Golden Legend* towards the close of the 13th century. Although there are some early wall paintings of St. Christopher, it was probably not until the 15th century that he became a really popular saint in England. It is likely that all the twenty-six medieval wall paintings of him in Suffolk are 15th century except for that at Fritton which is late 14th century. Moreover in the whole of England there are only eight churches of medieval foundation dedicated to St. Christopher, suggesting that, in early medieval times when parishes were being formed, though well known, he was not a very popular saint. Again, of nearly twenty monuments in English churches showing St. Christopher, only one, a brass of 1337 at Higham Ferrers in Northamptonshire, antedates 1450. Very rarely is any scene in the saint's life shown other than the Saint carrying the Christ Child across the river. The one exception in Suffolk is in the glass at Nowton, most of it of Flemish origin. In addition to the normal Christ-bearing scene, St. Christopher is shown kneeling before a crucifix hanging from a tree, and he is also shown being tortured. Christopher, so the legend goes, was a strong, active, uneducated man not given to prayer or religious contemplation, so that, after his conversion and on the advice of the hermit so

St Christopher. Stained glass at Norton.

often seen in paintings of the saint, he served Christ by carrying travellers across a dangerous ford. One wild and stormy night Christopher carried a little Child across the river, who, small though he was, was as 'hevy as leed'. When he set his small but weighty burden down Christopher wonderingly asked the Child why he was so heavy. 'Chylde, thou has put me in grete peryl, thou wayest alle most as I had had alle the world upon me, I might bere no greter burdon', to which the reply was 'Crystofre merveyle the nothing, for thou has not only born alle the world upon the, but thou hast born him that created and made alle the world upon thy sholdres'. Generally the giant figure of the saint is painted on the wall opposite the main door so that a traveller hastily opening the door could gaze on the saint, say a short prayer and go on his way reassured. It is easy to see how St. Christopher became the patron saint of travellers – even today a car dashboard may well sport a medallion of the saint. If St. Christopher protected the Christ Child in his travels he could equally well protect ordinary man on his journeyings. A wall painting of the saint at Creeting St. Peter has a scroll inscribed 'Christopheri sancti speciem quicumque tuetur illa nempe die nullo languore gravetur' (whoever looks at the picture of St. Christopher shall of a surety be burdened with no weariness on that day). Much of the interest of St. Christopher wall-paintings lies in the background scene on either bank, a medieval post windmill, a fisherman, the hermit holding his lantern, a town or village, while the river itself is chock full of fish of one kind or another. The fishermen on the bank should have no difficulty in making a good catch! Unfortunately the St. Christophers in Suffolk are often incomplete and show little of this background scene. Grundisburgh is an exception. In 1969 the Vatican reduced the cult of St. Christopher to one of merely local status.

Wallpaintings of St. Christopher are to be found at Alpheton, Barnby, Barsham, Belton (very faint), Bradfield Combust, Chediston, Chelsworth, Creeting St. Peter, Fritton, Grundisburgh, Hessett (two), Hintlesham, Hoxne, Kentford, Martlesham, Middleton, Mutford, Naughton, Risby (staff and hand only), Stradishall, Stowlangtoft, Troston, Little Wenham, Wilby and Worlingworth (feet only) to which must be added the late Sir Ninian Comper's early 20th century painting at Lound where an aeroplane and motor car replaced the traditional medieval accompaniments. In addition St. Christopher is found in old stained glass at Norton, Oakley and, as already mentioned, in Flemish glass at Nowton.

The Head of St. Edmund guarded by a wolf on a bench end at Hadleigh.

ST. EDMUND

Edmund became King of East Anglia in 855 and was crowned on Christmas Day at Bures, a royal vill in South Suffolk. In 869 he led an army against the invading Danes and was defeated. Edmund himself was captured, refused to renounce his Christian faith, was scourged, tied to a tree and shot at with arrows and finally beheaded, his martyrdom taking place on November 20. His body rested in a wooden chapel near the site of his martyrdom for 33 years and was then removed to Beodricsworth, now Bury St. Edmunds, where in 925 King Athelstan founded a small monastic community to look after the shrine. Further Danish raids led to the temporary removal of Edmund's body to London in 1010. By 1013 conditions were such that the body could be returned to Bury and during the journey it rested one night in the church of Greensted near Chipping Ongar in Essex where the log cabin type of wooden nave still remains, a unique survival in England. This is not the place to write of the subsequent history of the great Benedictine abbey of Bury St. Edmunds. Suffice it to add that a great deal of ink has been used in discussing whether St Edmund lies in an undiscovered grave at Bury or whether in 1216 the troops of Prince Louis of France, who had sided with the rebels against King John, stole St. Edmund's bones which were eventually deposited at St. Sernin's, Toulouse in France. The odds seem to favour the former theory.

The details of St. Edmund's death were told many years later to King Athelstan by Edmund's armour bearer who witnessed the events. St. Dunstan, then a young man of about twenty, was present on this occasion and about three years before his own death he told the story to Abbo of Fleury who included it in his *Passion of St. Edmund.* In this account the place of Edmund's martyrdom is given as Haegelisdun which philologists say cannot be equated with Hoxne, the traditional site of his martyrdom, which may have taken place at Hellesdon, just outside Norwich. A more recent claimant is a field in the parish of Bradfield St. Clare, six miles south of Bury, which is marked as Hellesdon on a tithe map of 1840 and near which is Sutton Hall. Hermann of Bury, writing at the end of the 11th century, records that Edmund was first buried at a chapel at Sutton.

Now what does legend or tradition tell us? On the road between Low Street and Cross Street, the two main hamlets of Hoxne, is Goldbrook Bridge, across a tributary of the River Dove. Tradition has it that after his defeat Edmund hid under an earlier bridge here and that he was betrayed to the Danes by a bridal couple passing over this bridge on their way to Hoxne Church. Edmund put a curse on all brides using this bridge on their way to their wedding and to this day some brides prefer to go by a longer route to Hoxne Church rather than risk the saint's curse. After his execution some of Edmund's followers soon found his body but it was only

Martyrdom of St. Edmund. Misericord at Norton.

after long searching that they came across his severed head guarded by a wild wolf. In a field between Goldbrook Bridge and Cross Street stands a stone cross which marks the site of a great and very ancient oak tree the collapse of which is recorded in the *Bury Post* for October 11th 1848. This was traditionally the tree to which St. Edmund was bound when he was shot at by the Danes and when the tree fell an arrow head was found embedded in it about five feet from the ground. The arrow head was known to exist up to the time of the break-up of the Hoxne estate in the 1920s, but its present whereabouts are unknown. Thus there are legends connecting Hoxne with St. Edmund but none connecting him with either Hellesdon near Norwich or Bradfield St. Clare. Moreover there were two chapels at Hoxne dedicated to St. Edmund at quite an early date. In 1098 Herbert de Losinga transferred the seat of his bishopric from Thetford to Norwich and in a charter of 1101 Hoxne was given to Norwich Cathedral Priory as part of its endowment. Certainly the Norwich charter is the earliest known reference associating Hoxne with St. Edmund. Was this a move to give Norwich an association with St. Edmunds at the expense of Bury?

Inevitably St. Edmund, as a national resistance leader against the Danes and one who chose martyrdom rather than renounce his Christian faith, became very popular in Suffolk though curiously only six medieval churches in the county are dedicated to him: Assington, Bromeswell, Fritton (now in Norfolk), Hargrave, Kessingland and Southwold. In Norfolk there are twenty-one medieval dedications to St. Edmund. The smaller number in Suffolk is probably an indication that already by 869 many Suffolk churches had their dedications.

St. Edmund is depicted in several churches, generally shown holding an arrow as on the screen panel paintings at Belstead, Eye, Kersey, Nayland and Somerleyton, also on a panel, repainted, apparently, as recently as 1953, now at Riddlesworth just across the border in Norfolk but formerly in the now ruined and overgrown church at Knettishall. St. Edmund is also found on the very beautiful early 14th century painted retable at Thornham Parva, in wall paintings at Boxford and Lakenheath and in 15th century glass at Long Melford. Elsewhere a carving shows the wolf guarding between its paws the head of St. Edmund as on bench ends at Hadleigh and (much mutilated) at Hoxne, on the modern bishop's throne at Bury Cathedral and on the base of a 15th century window inserted into the front of Moyse's Hall, the 12th century house in the Market Place at Bury St. Edmunds. In a 15th century glass roundel at Hawstead the tree forms the centre-piece, with Edmund's crowned head to the left and to the right the wolf with 'heer, heer, heer' inscribed beneath showing how the wolf attracted the attention of the King's followers when they were searching for his head. Some versions claim it was the King's head itself which uttered the words.

The actual martyrdom itself is shown in a rather fragmentary wall painting at Troston and in another at Fritton where the wolf is already waiting to take charge of the head, also on a misericord at Norton where, bound to a tree, he is being shot at by three archers while a fourth rests his bow. Southwold Church is dedicated to St. Edmund and outside, above the great west window, is a stone inscription let into the flintwork which reads 'Sct Edmund ora p'nobis' (St. Edmund, pray for us). Each letter is crowned. The glass in the east window was destroyed in the last war. The present glass was designed by Sir Ninian Comper in 1954 and was his last work. It depicts Edmund before the Danish king who holds a large scimitar, Edmund being shot at and his Translation to Heaven. In the window on the north side of the sanctuary is an etched figure of St. Edmund bound fast to a tree. This work of John Hutton in 1971 is in memory of Lady Tennyson.

ST. EDWARD THE CONFESSOR

Edward the Confessor was King of England from 1042 till his death in 1066. Historians differ in their assessment of his ability as a king in a time of uncertainty as to the future of the country but his contemporaries noted 'his artless piety and simple goodness' and 'remembered with affection the dignified, kindly, gentle old man with rosy cheeks and long milk-white beard – he was apparently an albino – who was always easy of access and given to charity and good works' (L. E. Tanner, *vide* Bibliography). Edward had rebuilt Westminster Abbey and died only a few days after its consecration which he had been too ill to attend. Edward's shrine survives in the Abbey where the cornice of the screen behind the high altar (completed in 1441) is carved with scenes from his life. As the Norman kings claimed the English throne through their descent from Edward they would obviously encourage any attempts to effect his canonisation and, after an unsuccessful attempt in 1139 in the turbulent reign of Stephen, this was finally achieved in 1161. Almost exactly a hundred years after Edward's death a new life of the saint king was written by Aildred, Abbot of Rievaulx Abbey in Yorkshire, and here for the first time is recorded the legend of the ring and the pilgrims. According to the *Golden Legend* version of the story Edward, already an old man, gave a ring to a beggar. Two years later two English pilgrims in the Holy Land met an old man who said he was St. John the Evangelist. He gave the pilgrims the ring, telling them to return it to their king with the warning that his death would take place in about six months' time. Local tradition has it that these pilgrims came from Ludlow in Shropshire and in the east window of St. John's Chapel in the Church there the whole story is told in eight scenes in 15th century glass ending with the two pilgrims being entertained by the civic authorities on their return to Ludlow. The popularity of this legend was such that Edward the Confessor is almost always depicted holding a ring and is thus shown on the wallpost of the 15th century roof in the nave of St. Mary's Church, Bury St. Edmunds, on screen panels at Eye (a youthful looking St. Edward, contrary to the legend), Nayland, Rattlesden, Somerleyton and Woodbridge, and in late 15th century glass at Long Melford. In 1930 M. R. James recorded at Boxford traces of a wall painting of a king which he thought might be Edward the Confessor. Was he referring to the painting (now perhaps clearer than in his day) of St. Edmund in the south chapel? J. C. Wall (see Bibliography) records that in 1863 a painting showing St. Edward giving the ring was discovered in 'an old house' at Bury St. Edmunds. It was Edward who granted the Abbey of Bury the right of jurisdiction over eight and a half hundreds in Suffolk as well as the important manor of Mildenhall. Until the 15th century when St. George became generally accepted as the patron saint of England, St. Edward the Confessor and St. Edmund were widely regarded as England's patrons and on the Wilton Diptych (*c.* 1380) they are shown, together with St. John the Baptist, presenting Richard II to the Virgin and Child. Suffolk has no medieval church dedicated to Edward the Confessor, but a vanished chapel at Badmondisfield Hall, Wickhambrook, is recorded as having been dedicated to him.

Church of St. Ethelbert, Falkenham. Etching by Henry Davy, 1843.

ST. ETHELBERT

In 794, soon after Ethelbert had succeeded his father on the throne of East Anglia, he paid a visit to Offa, King of Mercia, at his palace near Hereford, ostensibly (and probably genuinely) to seek in marriage the hand of Aelfthryth, Offa's youngest daughter. Had the marriage taken place it would have brought East Anglia within the orbit of Mercia, surely a desirable aim from Offa's point of view. Why then was Ethelbert murdered? The words of a hymn which was sung at Hereford Cathedral on the anniversary of his death (May 20) suggest that Offa's queen Cynethryth had been attracted by Ethelbert who had resisted her advances and in revenge she had persuaded Offa that the real object of Ethelbert's visit was to spy out the land (but for what purpose?) and so he was murdered. One of the figures on the west front of Wells Cathedral shows a king standing on a woman. This has generally been accepted as representing Ethelbert trampling on Cynethryth. Offa's subsequent remorse for this murder may well have influenced his decision to go on pilgrimage to Rome and to found St. Alban's Abbey. Ethelbert had been buried at Marden, just north of Hereford, but his remains were subsequently translated to Hereford Cathedral which is dedicated jointly to St. Mary and St. Ethelbert. Here he is figured in medieval glass, brass and stone, as well as in painting on the new reredos (1951) in the Lady Chapel. There are also a St. Ethelbert's Hospital and a St. Ethelbert's Cross at Hereford, both 14th century in origin. Inevitably Ethelbert was also revered in East Anglia. He has dedications in Suffolk at Falkenham, Herringswell, Hessett and Tannington and (formerly) at Burstall and Hoxne. Seven Norfolk churches were dedicated to him (four survive) as well as five or six churches elsewhere (*e.g.* Little Dean in Gloucestershire). St. Ethelbert is figured on the screen dated 1458 at Burnham Norton in Norfolk but no medieval representation of him survives in Suffolk.

St. Ethelreda (probably). Stained glass at Norton.

ST. ETHELDREDA

St. Etheldreda is most closely associated with Ely. She was probably born at Exning near Newmarket and was the daughter of Anna, King of East Anglia. In 660 she married Egfrith, son of Oswy, King of Northumbria, but in 672 she left her husband, retired for a year to a nunnery at Coldingham near Berwick-on-Tweed and then came south and founded a monastery at Ely for both men and women (a fairly common practice at that date) which, after destruction by the Danes a century earlier, was refounded in 970 as a monastery for monks only which (by a practice almost unique to England) became a Cathedral in 1109. St. Etheldreda died of plague in 679. Scenes from her life are carved on the interior of the 14th century octagon at Ely. The name Etheldreda became mongrelised to Audrey and at St. Audrey's Fair 'taudry lace' of such poor quality was sold that it is said to have given origin to the word 'tawdry'.

St. Etheldreda is to be found in 15th century glass at Norton Church (though I think the identity is not certain), also on a screen panel at Westhall. Two figures carved on one of the 15th century priest's stalls at Blythburgh are said to be St. Etheldreda and Anna her father. He holds an orb in his left hand while his right is raised in blessing. She is crowned and her hands are together as if in prayer. This traditional attribution may well be correct. King Anna and Jurmin (traditionally the King's son and subsequently canonised) were probably buried in an earlier church here after their defeat in battle against the Danes in 654. Jurmin's body was in 1095 transferred to Bury Abbey where a shrine was erected in his honour.

Rumburgh Priory Church in 1791.

Blythburgh. Reconstruction by Hamlet Watling of window to St. Felix.

Redwald, King of East Anglia, who is the most likely occupant of the Sutton Hoo Ship Burial, became at least a nominal Christian though at the same time he continued to worship heathen Gods. He died in 624 or 625 and was succeeded by his son Eorpwald who was murdered in 628 shortly after his conversion. So Christianity was not well established in East Anglia till the time of Felix and Sigeberht.

Felix was born and educated in Burgundy. He came to England and worked under Archbishop Honorius at Canterbury. In 630 Sigeberht returned from his exile in Gaul and was crowned King of East Anglia. Felix then came to East Anglia and became bishop of a place Bede calls Domnoc. This has generally (and probably correctly) been identified with Dunwich but recently attempts have been made to equate Domnoc with Walton (near Felixstowe) where there was a priory church with the uncommon dedication of St. Felix. There was a Roman coastal fort at Walton and it is true that other early churches were founded within the walls of the Roman forts of the Saxon Shore – Reculver and Richborough in Kent, a church established at Burgh Castle by Felix's contemporary the Irish missionary St. Fursey, and Othona in Essex, now Bradwell-on-Sea, where the nave of Cedd's 7th century church miraculously survives. The rival claims of Dunwich and Walton to be identified with Domnoc will probably never be settled if only because both sites now lie beneath the sea.

What about the suggestive name of Felixstowe? This is by tradition the place where Felix landed when he came over from Kent. If he did come by sea this would be a sensible place to land and it was not too far from the royal palace at Rendlesham. But the name Felixstowe is not found before the 16th century. In the 14th century it is recorded as Fylthestowe.

Felix's missionary work achieved considerable success and was given every encouragement by King Sigeberht who during his exile had become a very devout convert to Christianity. Sometime after 641 Sigeberht was killed in battle against Penda of Mercia. However, Felix was fully supported by King Anna, an ardent Christian, three of whose daughters became saints, Etheldreda, Saxburga and Werburga. Felix died in 647 at Domnoc and was first buried at Soham just south of Ely. His final resting place was at Ramsey Abbey in Huntingdonshire (now part of Cambridgeshire).

Considering that Felix did such outstanding work in propagating the gospel in East Anglia it is surprising how little impact he appears to have made in the later Middle Ages. Apart from the destroyed priory at Walton he has only one other dedication in Suffolk and this is at Rumburgh which he shares with St. Michael. I know of only one medieval representation of him in a Suffolk church, at Blythburgh in 15th century glass which is inscribed *S. Felix* so there is no doubt as to its identity.

St. George and the Dragon. Chest at Southwold.

ST. GEORGE

St. George was a native of Palestine, the son of wealthy parents. It is almost certain that he was a soldier who served with distinction in the Roman army, but he became a Christian, refused to worship heathen gods and was martyred, probably about the year 303, at Lydda in Palestine and was buried there. This is the story to which legends were added. The story of St. George and the Dragon was invented to make St. George the symbol of Good overcoming Evil. According to this story the city of Silene in Libya was terrorised by a great dragon who lived in a lake and demanded two sheep a day for its food. When the supply of sheep ran out a human victim was each day chosen by lot, and thus one day the king's daughter became the next victim. As, dressed as a bride, she went to meet her death, a young man on horseback approached her and on hearing the reason for her sadness he rode towards the dragon and so wounded it that it became harmless. George then told the princess to throw her girdle round the dragon's neck and lead it into the city. After the royal family and the citizens had been converted the dragon was slain. This legend became very popular through its inclusion in *The Golden Legend.*

Naturally this story of St. George appealed to soldiers. He was known in England at quite an early date (Bede makes mention of him) but he only became really popular in England as a result of the Crusades, for in the First Crusade the English army was encouraged at the siege of Antioch (1098) by a vision of St. George, shortly after which the city fell into their hands. He also came to the aid of the Crusaders under Richard Coeur de Lion at the siege of Acre in the Third Crusade and transformed near-defeat into victory. Thus it is not surprising that St. George replaced Edward the Confessor and St. Edmund as patron saint of England. In 1969 the Vatican reduced the cult of St. George to one of merely local status.

Sometimes St. George and the Dragon are shown alone with no subsidiary details as in the early 15th century wall painting at Bradfield Combust where rather awkwardly St. George spears the dragon with his left hand while he wields a sword with his right. The cross of St. George appears prominently on his breast plate. He is given a rather eastern appearance by the great bunch of feathers surmounting his helmet and his long scarf blown by the wind. Elsewhere a wealth of detail is inserted including the king and queen watching events from the battlements of the city. Such a painting was that on the south wall of the nave at Kersey, first uncovered in 1887 but now almost obliterated. It was much clearer when I first saw it about 1935 when, among other details, a post windmill was quite distinct. At Troston there are traces of two wallpaintings of St. George. The earlier, a smaller and rather lifeless one, dates from about 1250. Further west is another painting of the same subject, about 200 years later in date, a far more vivid and lifelike picture. There is the

St. Helen's Church Ipswich from Ogilby's map of the town 1674, engraved 1698.

outline of a wall painting in the south transept of Earl Stonham depicting St. George and the dragon. A rather bucolic looking king is watching events from a turret on the town wall. Paintings of St. George have also been recorded at Bramfield, Chelsworth, Preston and Sproughton but they are no longer visible. He is carved on the font at Stowlangtoft and in mortal combat with the dragon in the spandrels of porch doorways at Alderton, Badwell Ash, Hessett, Palgrave, Parham, Sweffling and Worlingworth, while in one of the spandrels of the north aisle roof at Mildenhall there is a splendid carving of St. George piercing the dragon, with the crowned king and queen watching events from the fortified city. Dangerously close to the rear hoofs of the horse kneels the princess with, on a leash, either a pet dog or (in anticipation) a diminutive dragon. St. George is also painted on the screen at Somerleyton and, in conflict with the dragon, is carved on the splendid early 15th century chest at Southwold and on a bench end at Withersfield, one of a rather crude set of poppy heads similar to those at Ickleton just across the border in Cambridgeshire. St. George in company with St. Michael figures in a memorial window put up in 1964 at Cockfield. Curiously only five medieval churches in Suffolk are dedicated to St. George, namely Bradfield St. George, South Elmham St. Cross, Shimpling, Thwaite and Wyverstone.

ST. HELEN

St. Helen or St. Helena was born about 250 in Bithynia. She married the Roman general Constantius Chlorus, but when he became Emperor he divorced her. Their son was Constantine, the first Christian Roman Emperor. St. Helen only became a Christian in old age. She went on pilgrimage to the Holy Land where she is credited with discovering the True Cross. Geoffrey of Monmouth, that rather inventive historian of the 12th century, declared that she was the daughter of Old King Coel, 'the merry old soul', legendary King and founder of Colchester. Hence her crowned figure holding the Cross and gazing towards Jerusalem was placed on top of the tower of the town hall of Colchester when it was completed in 1902. St. Helena is recognisable in art because she holds the True Cross. Thus she is depicted on the screen in Eye Church and (though the identification is not absolutely certain) in 14th century glass in Herringfleet Church. She also figures on the Victorian stone reredos at Bramfield. She has only one medieval dedication in Suffolk, a church in Ipswich.

St. James the Great. Screen painting at Southwold.

ST. JAMES THE GREAT

Anselm, Abbot of Bury St. Edmunds from 1121 to 1148, had vowed to go on pilgrimage to the shrine of St. James at Santiago de Compostela in the north-west corner of Spain. For various reasons he was unable to carry out his vow and in atonement he built the parish church of St. James, which eventually became the Cathedral of the diocese of St. Edmundsbury and Ipswich in 1914. Apart from the detached bell tower, the present church is, of course, of much later date than Abbot Anselm's time, the nave being attributable to William Wastell who died at Bury in 1515 and who was the master mason responsible for some of the work at King's College Chapel and Great St. Mary's at Cambridge, the Bell Harry (central) tower at Canterbury, the 'New Building' at Peterborough Abbey (now the Cathedral), Saffron Walden Church and, by analogy, almost certainly the naves of Lavenham Church and Isleham (Cambs.). The west front of the Cathedral at Bury is decorated, *inter alia*, with the staff, wallet and scallop shell of St. James, the staff and wallet signifying the pilgrim and the scallop shell the symbol that one had been on pilgrimage to Santiago. St. James can always be identified by the scallop shell on his cap or wallet. He is said to have brought Christianity to Spain and then to have been martyred by Herod Agrippa, thus being the first apostle to have died for his faith. He was also the great supporter of the Christians in their fight to turn the Moors out of Spain. Subsequently his relics are reputed to have been brought to Santiago where his shrine is still a great centre of pilgrimage. There one can perhaps sense more than anywhere else in Europe the full feeling of medieval Christianity.

In addition to the present Cathedral at Bury, Suffolk churches at Icklingham, Nayland, South Elmham and Stanstead are dedicated to him, as is also the now ruined chapel of a former leper hospital at Dunwich. St. James is painted as a pilgrim with staff and scallop shell on the screens at Southwold, Westhall and Woodbridge and with scallop shell only at Hasketon and there are faint traces of a wall painting of him at Belton. The figure facing east on the shaft of the font at Wilby looks as if he is holding a scallop shell. If so he is St. James. With staff and wallet he is carved with the other apostles on the front of the choir stalls at Blythburgh. Munro Cautley thought this carving formed the front of the rood screen in pre-Reformation days; it might have been the front of the rood loft. St. James is also depicted in modern glass (1973) in the east window at Boxford and on a 15th century bench end at Athelington.

Sir John Schorne. Painted screen panel formerly in St. Gregory's Church, Sudbury, now at Gainsborough's House, Sudbury.

SIR JOHN SCHORNE

John Schorne was rector first of Monks Risborough, then of North Marston, both in Buckinghamshire. At the latter village he is credited with having struck the earth in a time of drought and so to have produced a much needed supply of water. A local jingle ran 'Master John Schorne, Gentleman born, Conjured the Devil into a boot' and it is in this act that he is depicted on a few Devon and Norfolk screens and in Suffolk on a solitary panel formerly in St. Gregory's Church, Sudbury but now at Gainsborough's House in the same town. The boot legend may well have been a pictorial expression of Sir John's ability to cure gout. He died about 1313 and although he was never officially canonised his relics brought in a sufficient flow of pilgrims for the chancel of North Marston Church to be rebuilt rather splendidly in the 15th century. This roused the jealousy of the Dean and Canons of Windsor who, some thirty miles to the south, were rebuilding St. George's Chapel at the Castle and needed relics to attract pilgrims and therefore money to the site. In April 1478, Pope Sixtus IV granted a 'Bulla pro Translatione Magistri Johannis Schorne' and in November 1479 Dunstable Priory presented the living of North Marston to the Dean and Canons of Windsor in exchange for that of Weedon Beck in Northamptonshire which Windsor owned. After that the translation presented no difficulties though it is curious that no representation of Sir John Schorne survives in St. George's Chapel.

The Abbey at Bury had a window to Schorne which was in private hands in the town when Hamlet Watling traced it in 1838. The 13 inch figure was tonsured, and held an open book in the left hand and a yellow and red book in the other from which the dragon-like devil was almost out, to the priest's obvious consternation. By the 1860s the glass was lost.

A 'fare prayer of Mr. John Schorne for ye Axes' (the ague) was discovered in Sloane MS 389 in the British Library in 1885. It is in Latin and in its course describes Schorne in eloquent detail: a good parish priest, a learned theologian, a renowned preacher, a holy man, a pattern to the clergy, a wonder worker, an illustrious physician to the body, a restorer of sight, a guide of pilgrims and endowed with many other virtues and graces.

St Margaret of Antioch ordered to stand in a vat of boiling oil. Stained glass at Combs.

ST. MARGARET OF ANTIOCH

Although there is no historical evidence of Margaret's existence she nevertheless became very popular in the later Middle Ages. Legend has it that she was the daughter of a heathen priest at Antioch, that because she was converted to Christianity her father turned her out of their home and she made a living minding sheep. Olybrius, who was governor of Antioch, wished to seduce or marry her but she refused. There followed many tortures such as being put into a vat of boiling oil and being swallowed by a dragon whose belly burst asunder so that she was saved. She and those she had converted were eventually beheaded in the persecution under Diocletian. Her popularity can be accounted for by the fact that she promised protection to those who prayed for her aid; women in childbirth, and those near to death.

Single figures of her can be recognised as she is generally shown spearing a dragon at her feet as on the corner post of the Fox and Goose Inn facing the churchyard at Fressingfield; this was formerly the Guildhall. The figure of Margaret is very worn but the dragon at her feet is better preserved and makes identity certain. Single figures of Margaret are also found on the font at Stowlangtoft, in 15th century glass at Norton, on bench ends at Athelington and Ufford, on panel paintings on the screens at Belstead and Westhall, in early 14th century wall painting at Little Wenham and on the very beautiful painted retable, also of the early 14th century, at Thornham Parva. But of greater interest is a series of scenes in the life of St. Margaret in 15th century glass at Combs Church near Stowmarket. Margaret is depicted first keeping her sheep while the governor Olybrius rides by; second, brought before Olybrius for interrogation (note on a pedestal the idol which Margaret was urged to worship); third, she is thrust through a portcullised gateway into her prison; fourth, in three scenes in one panel, Margaret is swallowed by the dragon, she emerges from the dragon, she beats the dragon; and fifth Margaret is about to step into a vat of burning oil. This scene has several interesting details. Margaret wears a blue skirt but her body is uncovered from the waist upwards. Not unnaturally she has raised her arms in protest. There are two men, one of whom is pitchforking wood to increase the strength of the fire. The details of the wooden vat are very clear. In the background is a typical East Anglian gabled house and beside it a portcullis, presumably guarding Margaret's prison. The series is probably incomplete as there would surely be at least one further panel showing Margaret's martyrdom. Wall paintings at Wissington were uncovered by Prof. E. W. Tristram in 1933 and these included faint traces of a series connected with St. Margaret, but hardly anything of these is now visible. At Risby a figure birching a devil is almost certainly St. Margaret, a scene from another series of wall paintings about the Saint. There are twenty medieval churches in Suffolk dedicated to St. Margaret, though in two cases (Chattisham and Pakefield), the dedication is shared with All Saints.

St. Michael. The Wenhaston Doom.

ST. MICHAEL

Michael is first mentioned in the Book of Daniel. Early on in the Christian era he is revealed as an angel of majestic appearance who has power to rescue souls from Hell, and this would account for his popularity (686 medieval churches in England are dedicated to him). Consequently he is often shown as weighing a soul on a balance with a devil trying but not succeeding in weighing down the pan containing the bad deeds of the soul being judged, while often the Virgin Mary is effectively using her influence on the pan with the soul's good deeds. In this form St. Michael often forms part of a Doom, nowhere more effectively than in the late 15th century Doom painting at Wenhaston. This was painted on boards which formed a tympanic filling to the chancel arch, presumably because there was not sufficient space between the original chancel arch and the roof for the more normal wall painting of this subject. The crucified Christ and the attendant figures of the Virgin Mary and St. John were in the round and the notches where they were fixed into the boarding are still visible. St. Michael in a red cloak stands to the right of the Cross, holding his drawn sword with his right hand and the balance with his left. A human soul is being weighed in the left pan while a devil unsuccessfully puts his whole weight on the right pan. Above, Christ sits on a rainbow in judgement as in the much cruder Doom painting at Stanningfield. The blessed are being admitted to Heaven in the bottom left hand corner and the damned are despatched to hell in the bottom right. At the Reformation the figures in relief were removed, the whole painting covered with whitewash. The Royal Arms were placed over it and to this date belongs the inscription underneath, the gist of which is 'obey those in authority or be damned'. In 1892 the chancel arch was rebuilt. The wooden tympanum was taken down and placed in the churchyard as lumber, but a heavy downpour of rain revealed traces of painting and, to the credit of the parochial authorities, the woodwork was taken back to the church and cleaned, so preserving for us the best of the four or five Dooms painted on wooden tympana surviving in this country. About 1970 the painting was carefully cleaned and treated by experts with the help of a Pilgrim Trust grant, and it is now considerably clearer than it was a few years ago.

At Long Melford there is in 15th century glass of the Norwich school, now in the north aisle, an incomplete inscription 'S'c'e Micha . . . '. Of the saint there only remains his head, part of a wing, three cords hanging from a hook originally attached to one of the pans in the scales and the hand which held the scales.

The roofs of Mildenhall Church are among the finest in Suffolk and particularly ornate are the carvings in the spandrels of the hammer beams in the north aisle. The west face of the easternmost spandrel shows a figure, almost certainly St. Michael, and a dragon. St. Michael with drawn sword about to slay the dragon is the left hand painted figure

St. Osyth in 19th century glass at Long Melford.

on the screen in Somerleyton Church balancing the figure of St. George at the opposite end of the screen. St. Michael and the dragon also occur among the screen panel paintings at Westhall, while at Southwold he is shown on the screen as the Archangel with sword. Rood loft staircases are often to be found in churches but very rarely does the wooden door to the lower entrance survive. There is one such at South Cove and on it is painted St. Michael slaying the dragon. St. Michael with his scales is carved on a 15th century poppy-head bench end at Withersfield, with the soul in one pan and devil in the other who stretches out his arm in a vain attempt to pull the beam of the scales down to his advantage. There is a wall painting at Cowlinge showing St. Michael weighing the souls. It is good to see that the good deeds always outweigh the bad. St. Michael and the Dragon feature in one of the medallions on a bell at Bromeswell, cast at Mechlin in 1530. Finally and earliest in date, in the north aisle of St. Nicholas' Church at Ipswich there is an 11th century carving of St. Michael and the Dragon inscribed 'Her Sanctus Michael Feht Wid Dame Dragon'. When in combat with the Dragon St. Michael is usually shown winged and so can be distinguished from St. George.

Fifteen Suffolk churches of medieval foundation are dedicated to St. Michael namely Benacre, Boulge (together with All Angels), Brantham, Cookley, one of the South Elmham churches, Framlingham, Hunston, Occold, Oulton, Peasenhall, Rendham, Rumburgh, Rushmere, Tunstall, and Woolverstone. Hilltop churches are often dedicated to St. Michael as with Mont Saint Michel in Normandy, St. Michael's Mount in Cornwall and Brentor in Devon. A modest parallel can perhaps be seen at Oulton Church where St. Michael's church broods above the ancient estuary of the Waveney.

ST. OSYTH

St. Osyth (or Osith) doesn't quite qualify as an East Anglian saint as the scene of her life centres round Chich or, as it later became known, St. Osyth in North-East Essex.

Osyth was unwillingly betrothed to Sighere, King of the East Saxons, but on the very day of the wedding Providence stepped in. Just before the ceremony took place it was reported that a wonderful white stag had been seen nearby. This was too much for the hunting instincts of Sighere who with his companions promptly rode off in pursuit. This gave Osyth the opportunity to slip away to a bishop who conveniently happened to be in the neighbourhood (or he may, of course, have come to the wedding) and who quickly professed her as a nun. At first Sighere was furious but he eventually relented sufficiently to give her the manor of Chich where she established a nunnery. In October, 653 (though sometimes a rather later

St. Peter and St. Paul. Modern sculpture in the south porch at Lavenham.

date is given) a band of Danes raided up the estuary to Chich where their leader tried to force Osyth to worship idols. She refused and was eventually beheaded whereupon she promptly got up and carried her head to the Church of St. Peter and St. Paul (presumably the predecessor of the present parish church of that dedication). She then collapsed. Most of the present buildings of St. Osyth Priory (refounded as a house of Augustinian canons about 1120) are a post-Reformation adaption for domestic purposes but the splendid gatehouse still survives. In 15th century glass at Long Melford there is a female figure in a long cloak carrying a crozier. Beside her is a similar figure but carrying her head. These two figures fairly certainly represent St. Osyth who is also shown, rather incorrectly, in 19th century glass in the same church. No medieval Suffolk church is dedicated to her.

ST. PETER AND ST. PAUL

I have dealt under one heading with these two saints as they are so often found together, being the two most important leaders of Christianity in its early days. No medieval church in Suffolk is dedicated to St. Paul on his own but there are fourteen churches with a joint dedication including Lavenham where figures of St. Peter and St. Paul have recently been placed in the niche in the south porch. These figures show how difficult it is, whatever their merits in their own right, to place modern figures in a medieval setting. St. Peter was obviously more popular than St. Paul because he held the keys of the gates of Heaven as so vividly portrayed in the Doom at Wenhaston (described under St. Michael) where, beautifully robed, he is vetting a king, a queen, a bishop and a cardinal before allowing them to pass through the gates. No fewer than fifty-three medieval churches in Suffolk are dedicated to St. Peter alone. These two saints are easily recognised as Peter is always shown holding keys while St. Paul has an unsheathed sword. Their life stories are too well known to need to be repeated here. Inevitably various apocryphal and traditional stories were circulated, one of the commonest being that St. Peter asked to be crucified upside down because, owing to his denial of Christ, he was unworthy to suffer death in the same way as his Master.

In Suffolk both St. Peter and St. Paul are painted on the screen at Southwold and the famous retable at Thornham Parva and are carved on the font at Stowlangtoft. St. Peter with key and St. Paul with sword are also carved on the front of the choir stalls at Blythburgh. On the screen at Eye, St. Paul is painted on the northernmost panel. The figure on the southernmost panel is so disfigured as to be unidentifiable but it may safely be taken to have been St. Peter.

In the fragmentary Doom painting above the chancel arch at Bacton St.

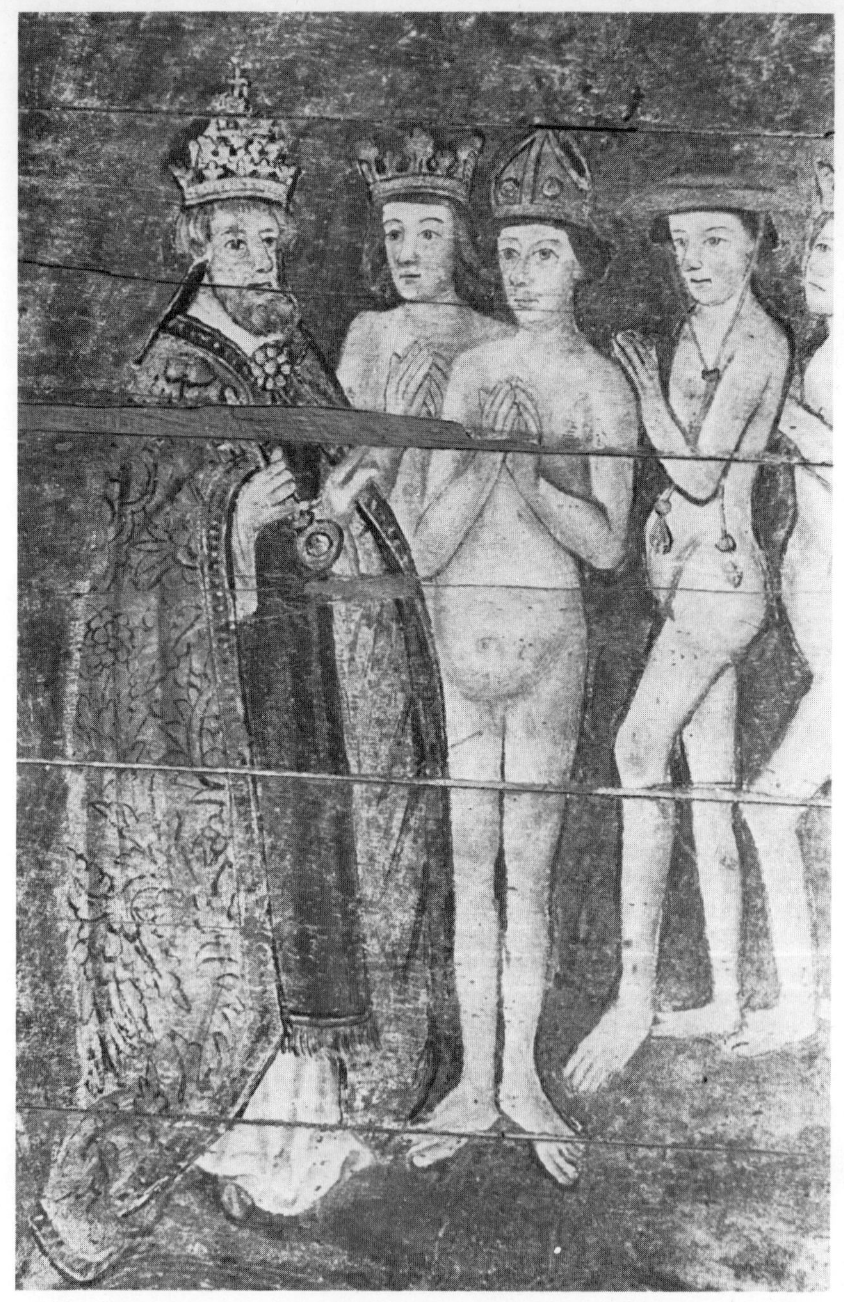

St. Peter. The Wenhaston Doom.

Peter is clearly visible holding his keys, as he also is on the much restored version at Chelsworth. A panel painting from the screen formerly in the ruined church at Knettishall but now in the Norfolk church of Riddlesworth and apparently repainted as recently as 1953, shows St. Peter wearing a papal tiara and, unusually, holding a church while the crossed keys are in the top right hand corner of the panel. At Thrandeston, St. Peter is carved on one of the bench ends. At Denston a medieval bell from the Bury foundry is inscribed with a prayer to St. Peter. The crossed keys of St. Peter are carved on the stone plinth or base of the tower at Lavenham and on benchwork at Fressingfield. St. Peter is also found in 15th century glass at Yaxley and Long Melford. St. Paul with sword is carved on a bench end at Athelington and holding a book and sword he is found on the west face of the shaft of the 15th century font at Wilby. St. Paul with sword is carved in one of the spandrels of the hammer beam roof at Heveningham. At Hessett there is the lower part of a panel of glass which showed St. Peter cutting off the ear of Malchus at the time of Christ's arrest. The scene is recognisable because of Malchus's lantern on the ground. St. Paul with sword (the head is obviously not original) is also found in old glass in the same church. In the 1540s the chancel at Framlingham was rebuilt on a large scale by the Howards, Dukes of Norfolk, who owned Framlingham Castle and who up to the Reformation had been buried at Thetford Priory. One of the splendid monuments at Framlingham commemorates Thomas Howard, 3rd Duke of Norfolk, who died in 1554. It is Renaissance in style and remarkably for that date the fourteen niches house figures of the twelve apostles (including, of course, St. Peter) and Paul and, for reasons which are obscure, Aaron. As the excellent guide book to the Church affirms 'these represent the last major display of religious imagery in England before the full weight of Reformation theology made such things impossible'.

St. Petronilla. Screen painting at Somerleyton.

ST. PETRONILLA

Petronilla became the legendary daughter of St. Peter in the 6th century because she was, in the first century, descended from the Emperor Vespasian's grandfather, Titus Flavius *Petro*. In Suffolk, Whepstead Church and the late 13th century chapel at Little Wenham Hall are dedicated to her, as was also a Hospital at Bury St. Edmunds, and a chapel in what is now Chapel Field beside the Ipswich-Bucklesham road. Otherwise she doesn't boast a single medieval dedication throughout the length and breadth of England. The four ribs of the quadripartite vault of the late 13th century chapel at Little Wenham Hall meet in a boss carved with a figure reputed to represent St. Petronilla. She is depicted on the screens at Litcham and North Elmham (both Norfolk) and Somerleyton. In all three cases she is shown holding a book and a key, the latter with reference to St. Peter. She seems to have enjoyed something of a cult in Suffolk. Thus David Dymond, in his guide to the two churches at Stanton, mentions that in 1590 Robert Sheparde, the then incumbent, recorded that 'in tyme past the Church called All Saintes had a Saint called St. Parnell standin in it, whereunto many resorted as Pilgrims and did offer and therof great gayne was made'. In pre-reformation days then, All Saints Church, Stanton, possessed a statue of St. Petronilla to which pilgrims came and the church benefitted considerably from their offerings. It is also known that there was a special chapel dedicated to St. Petronilla in 1340 in that church, probably in the south aisle.

The remains of St. Petronilla were brought from the catacombs and were buried in a circular chapel on the south side of old St. Peter's in Rome, but were removed in 1612 to a chapel near the east end of the present St. Peter's. But the Abbey at Bury claimed to possess her skull, said to be efficacious in case of headaches, and this may account for her minor cult in West Suffolk.

ST. THOMAS OF CANTERBURY

Thomas Becket was born in 1118 and was educated at Merton Abbey in Surrey and at Paris. He took minor orders and joined the household of Theobald, Archbishop of Canterbury. He also went abroad to study canon law at Bologna and Auxerre. Soon after he came to the throne in 1154, Henry II appointed Thomas Chancellor of England, and the two of them became very close friends. In 1161 Henry persuaded Thomas to become Archbishop of Canterbury on Theobald's death. Now all was changed and Thomas became the unswerving advocate and supporter of the Church, when necessary against the King. Things had reached such a

Murder of St. Thomas Becket. Misericord at Fornham St. Martin.

pitch by 1164 that Thomas fled to France, staying first at Pontigny Abbey and then at Sens where in the Cathedral Treasury his chasuble and stole are still preserved. In 1170 a reconciliation was achieved between the King and the Archbishop and Thomas returned to Canterbury, having first excommunicated the Archbishop of York for crowning the King's eldest son, Henry, at Westminster Abbey. All schoolboys know of the King's rashly spoken words, 'Will no one rid me of this low-born priest?', how four of his knights subsequently murdered Thomas in his own Cathedral and Henry's subsequent penance walking barefoot through the snow. A wave of horror swept through Christendom and Thomas was canonised in 1173, but the relations in England between Church and State were affected less than might have been expected.

Thomas's shrine in Canterbury Cathedral became the most popular in England. Everyone has heard of Chaucer's pilgrims, journeying from London to Canterbury. The myth that pilgrims also used the prehistoric trackway called the Pilgrims' Way from Winchester to Canterbury has long been proved false though it is still far too frequently repeated, sometimes by writers who should know better.

St. Thomas's popularity as a saint took Europe by storm. Early in the 13th century at Sens and Chartres the whole story leading up to the martyrdom and the martyrdom itself was depicted in a series of glass panels. At Monreale in Sicily a mosaic of St. Thomas dates from before the end of the 12th century. Coming nearer home, five scenes of the martyrdom story are shown in the 15th century bosses of the north walk of the cloister at Norwich Cathedral. In Suffolk there is less to show, but at Fornham St. Martin there is a misericord with a remarkable carving of the Martyrdom. The tonsured Archbishop is kneeling before the altar, while behind him are two of the knights (there was obviously no room to show all four), both with drawn swords, the foremost in the act of cleaving the Archbishop's skull. Behind the altar is a single figure holding a crozier, obviously the faithful Edward Grim, who nearly had his arm severed from one of the sword cuts of the knights. Standing figures of archbishops on 15th century screen panels at Nayland and Somerleyton can fairly safely be identified as St. Thomas of Canterbury. A large wall painting of an ecclesiastic at Risby is probably early 12th century and so too early to be St. Thomas. A wall painting of the martyrdom on the south wall of Honington Church has only recently disappeared. On the splay of a window at Fritton Church there is a painting of St. Thomas which can be dated to about 1400. Little Welnetham is the only medieval church in Suffolk dedicated to St. Thomas of Canterbury, but by the time of his martyrdom (1170) most medieval parishes had already been formed.

ST. URSULA

Ursula, who is said to have lived in the 4th century, was the daughter of a British, possibly Cornish, king who was a Christian. She was betrothed to a heathen prince, but was allowed to remain unmarried for three years. This time she spent voyaging round the seas of Europe accompanied by ten other virgins, the eleven being increased to 11,000, probably as the result of a clerical error in the 10th century. They finally ended up at Cologne where they were martyred by the Huns, her companions being executed while Ursula herelf was shot at by the prince of the Huns, which is why she is sometimes shown holding an arrow like St. Edmund. Naturally her cult became mainly centred on Cologne, where Ursula and her companions were buried in a great church dedicated to her, but, because of her British origin she was also quite popular in England. With a crowd of maidens beneath her cloak she is depicted on the screens at Belstead, Eye, Kessingland (though too defaced to make identity certain) and Woodbridge, also in a 15th century stained glass roundel at South Elmham All Saints. No medieval church in Suffolk or indeed in the whole of England is dedicated to her.

ST. WILLIAM OF NORWICH

The aim of any great church whether it was secular or monastic, was by one means or another (and sometimes the means were pretty shady by our standards) to acquire the relics of a saint, because relics meant pilgrims and pilgrims meant offerings. Norwich Cathedral is still largely a 12th century Romanesque building and one reason why the monks there lacked sufficient funds to carry out rebuilding on a large scale may well have been that the relics of St. William could not possibly hope to compete in popularity with the neighbouring shrines of Our Lady at Walsingham and of St. Edmund at Bury, the former probably second only in popularity in England to the shrine of St. Thomas at Canterbury. What hope was there that the relics of St. William, the boy said to have been murdered by the Jews at Norwich, could rival these national shrines? Indeed there is strong evidence that the cult of St. William was purely a local one. He is not depicted in any medieval church outside East Anglia. St. William is shown on the screen at Eye, a boylike figure holding a cross and three nails, while one of the figures on the screen at Somerleyton may also possibly be him.

In 1715 Dr. Henry Colman, Fellow of Trinity College, Cambridge, founded a parish library at Brent Eleigh. This was originally housed in a building added to the east end of the church but it was pulled down about 1857 and the library was moved to a small building in the north-east corner of the churchyard. Here one day in 1890 it was inspected by Dr. M. R. James, Provost of Eton, writer of inimitable ghost stories and perhaps our greatest authority to date on medieval hagiology and iconography. He had had Suffolk connections from childhood, for his father had been rector of Great Livermere. Among the contents of the library (subsequently removed to the University Library and the Fitzwilliam at Cambridge) Dr. James found a manuscript of the Life and Miracles of St. William written by Thomas of Monmouth, a Norwich monk, about 1172, less than thirty years after St. William's supposed martyrdom in 1144. By medieval standards Thomas's account is remarkably fair and well balanced, but he devotes only one out of seven sections to the life and death of William. The story is briefly this. At the age of eight William worked with a skinner, first near his home at Haveringland six miles north-west of Norwich, and then in Norwich itself. Here he met and became friendly with several Jewish customers. On Monday in Passion Week 1144 William was offered a position under the cook of William, Archdeacon of Norwich. In spite of opposition from his mother and aunt (his father was already dead) the boy accepted but on the way to his new post he was enticed into a Jewish house. Here on the next day, which was the Jewish Passover, William was murdered by having one foot and one arm tied and the other foot and arm nailed to a gallows as depicted on the screen at Loddon, just across the border in Norfolk. On Good Friday the body was taken in a sack to Thorpe Wood for burial but the party met a prominent citizen of Norwich named Aelward Ded whose suspicions were aroused. However, the body was buried, and with the help of John the Sheriff who had always been friendly to the Jews, Aelward took an oath of silence regarding his suspicions which he only broke on his deathbed five years later. On Easter Saturday the body was discovered and when signs of torture were observed the crime was immediately laid at the feet of the Jews. Here was an opportunity too good to be missed and on April 24 the body was given burial first in the monks' cemetery and then in the Cathedral itself.

INDEX OF PLACES IN SUFFOLK

NOTES

NOTES

NOTES